Violin
Basics

by Paul Harris & Jessica O'Leary

With illustrations by Bill Jones

Backing tracks are available
by scanning the QR code:

or from fabermusic.com/audio

Contents

A message to you

Welcome to **Violin Basics**, the exciting way to learn the violin. Before you begin, here are some ideas to make sure you get the most out of your violin playing!

- Ask your teacher if there is anything you're not quite sure about or if your strings go out of tune.

- Always use the backing tracks (X) when you can. These can be accessed by scanning the QR code or downloading from **fabermusic. com/audio**. If you want to change the speed of a track there are many programmes available online to do this.

- Get together with other musician friends – there are lots of duets in the teacher's book that you can enjoy together and they will prepare you for playing in ensembles and orchestras.

Try to practise regularly – it's the time when you do most of your learning! Do as much as you want to – don't set yourself limits. It's useful to practise at the same time every day when you concentrate best and if you include the '4 Ps' in every session, you'll make excellent progress.

- **Posture** Check every time you play that your violin is resting in a comfortable position on your collarbone (not your chest) and supported by the weight of your head. Don't forget to pop on your shoulder rest or sponge if you use one. Point the violin at the left-hand side of the music, which should be at eye level, and stand in a relaxed way.

- **Pulse** Always (and we mean always!) count yourself in (one or two bars) loudly in your head before you begin every piece. The difference will be immense and understanding rhythm will never be a problem.

- **Phonology** This is just a fancy word for sound! Listen to the sound you make – is it the best you can? Hold the bow with curled fingers and thumb in a relaxed way, keeping your little finger on the top. Use lots of bow to make a confident sound and check that your bow is parallel to the bridge and not skidding.

- **Personality (of the music)** Are you always putting character into your pieces? When you can, are you putting lots of contrasts into the dynamics levels?

Enjoy your violin playing – you are setting off on a wonderful and exciting journey that will give you a skill to last you all your life!

With great thanks to Helen Dromey, Lizzie MacCarthy and Jonathan Whiting.

© 2020 by Faber Music Ltd
This edition first published in 2020
Bloomsbury House
74–77 Great Russell Street
London WC1B 3DA

Music processed by Donald Thomson
Text designed by Elizabeth Ogden and Susan Clarke
Cover design by Chloë Alexander Design
Printed in England by Caligraving Ltd
All rights reserved

ISBN10: 0-571-54180-1
EAN13: 978-0-571-54180-5

To buy Faber Music publications or to find out about the full range of titles available please contact your local music retailer or Faber Music sales enquiries:

Faber Music Limited, Burnt Mill, Elizabeth Way, Harlow, CM20 2HX England
Tel: +44 (0) 1279 82 89 82
fabermusic.com

A message to your parent or teacher

This tutor is designed to take students from day one to Grade one. It is based on a number of principles that have emerged from our own experiences as teachers, from sharing ideas with fellow teachers and from observing the reactions of the pupils we have had the pleasure to teach. Young players like and respond positively to structured, imaginative and methodical teaching. They also:

- prefer catchy tunes to exercises and studies
- would rather be entertained than lectured
- enjoy fun titles
- learn best what they want to know or what they need to know
- like to laugh.

We have tried our best to follow these principles!

New elements are introduced and then reinforced in a logical and uncluttered fashion. There are, of course, exercises and studies but these are carefully disguised and there is a broad mixture of newly composed music together with old favourites and popular tunes.

We have tried not to get in the way of the teacher but instead provide a method that both pupil and teacher can enjoy together. A mix of piano accompaniments (🎹) and violin duet parts (👥) are available in the teacher's book and online backing tracks of the piano accompaniments can be found on **fabermusic.com/audio** or via the QR code.

If you want to change the tempo (speed) of a track, there are free programmes available online.

Initial stages are crucial in setting up the posture correctly. Spending time on the games provided will reinforce important technical control while keeping the posture relaxed, fingers curled and bow parallel to the bridge. These elements will need to be checked every time a pupil plays in order to ensure smooth progress.

In this book, we set up the core skills for seamless progress and often refer to the **'high dot'**. This is placed exactly halfway between the bridge and the nut. **Please put a sticky dot on the fingerboard under the A string to mark the position** (as shown on page 5). Moving around the violin from the beginning stages will give excellent posture, a flexible technique and remove any anxiety later on about shifting.

Do remember that nails need to be kept short and it is important to check posture frequently. The violin will need to be tuned regularly and the angle and height of the shoulder rest (if used) checked by the teacher.

We hope that this tutor will make playing music a hugely enjoyable experience.

Paul Harris and Jessica O'Leary

Your violin and bow

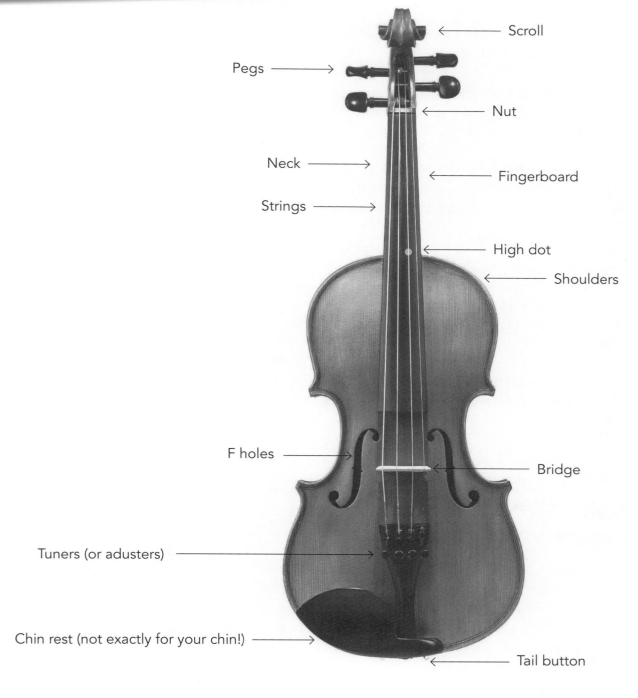

Scroll

Pegs

Nut

Neck

Fingerboard

Strings

High dot

Shoulders

F holes

Bridge

Tuners (or adusters)

Chin rest (not exactly for your chin!)

Tail button

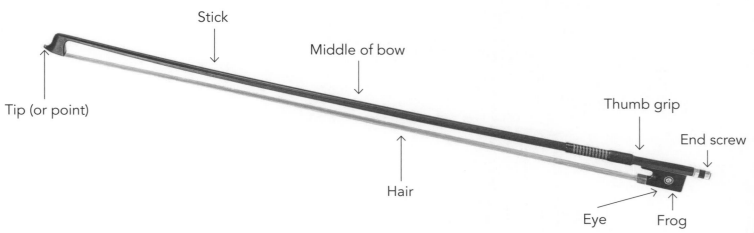

Stick

Middle of bow

Tip (or point)

Thumb grip

End screw

Hair

Eye

Frog

Holding the violin

- Stand with your feet shoulder-width apart and in a relaxed position.

- Begin with the back of the violin facing you and put your left hand over the left shoulder of the violin so your fingers cover all the strings near the high dot.

- Hold the violin to the left in a 'superhero' pose with your right hand supporting the tail button.

- Turn the violin, lift up your head and pop it on to your left collarbone.

- Your left hand will stay in that position for the plucking pieces and any pieces that use the high dot.

The violin needs something to stop it slipping and your teacher may suggest a shoulder rest, sponge, pad or thin cloth.

Quick check every time before you play

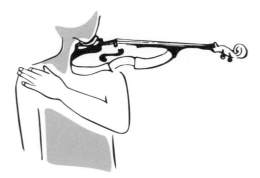

Balancing the violin firmly with the side of your chin, release your left hand and reach over to tap your right shoulder.

Fun fact

The 'chin rest' is actually for the left side of your chin. It makes balancing the violin between your collarbone, chin and hand more comfortable.

Holding the bow

- With the bow parallel to the floor, hold it at the balance point of the stick with your **left** hand.

- The point of the bow will be to the left, and the hair should face a little towards you (but don't touch it!).

- Hover your right hand over the heel of the bow and 'wave' your right hand up and down.

- Now place your right fingers on to the stick at the heel with your thumb curved. Your two middle fingers go over the stick, opposite the thumb.

- There should be small gaps between the first and second finger and the third and little finger, which is the only one that goes on top of the stick!

Quick check every time before you play: finger tapping

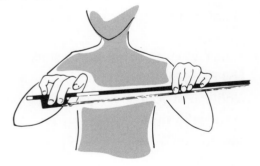

With your left hand holding the bow stick at the balance point and best bow hold with your right hand, lift your bow-hand first finger up and down eight times. Then lift your little finger eight times, making sure it lands on the **top** of the stick each time. Finally, lift and replace both middle fingers together eight times.

Rest position, performing and taking a bow

You'll notice that violinists use a bow *and* take a bow!

Rest position

Always put your violin and bow in rest position when you are listening to your teacher, waiting to play or taking a bow. It is a way of relaxing your arms while keeping your instrument safe.

- With feet together and your **left** hand near the high dot, pop your violin under your **right** arm, keeping the elbow behind the bridge so you don't get rosin on your sleeve.

- Point your bow across your knees but don't bump it on the floor!

- When you are ready to play, move your right elbow out a little to release the violin so you don't pull off your shoulder rest.

Performing and taking a bow

Performing is fun, so play a lot to your family, friends and pets! This is how to get ready:

- In **rest position**, announce the name of your piece and stand with feet shoulder-width apart.

- Place your violin on your shoulder and prepare your bow hold.

- Play the piece with great character!

- At the end, go back to rest position and prepare to take a bow. Bowing is very important – it is your way of thanking your audience for listening.

- Look at your audience and smile. Then bow, by bending forward from your waist while looking at your shoes. It's useful to have words like 'hello shoes' to say in your head before you straighten up again.

Open strings

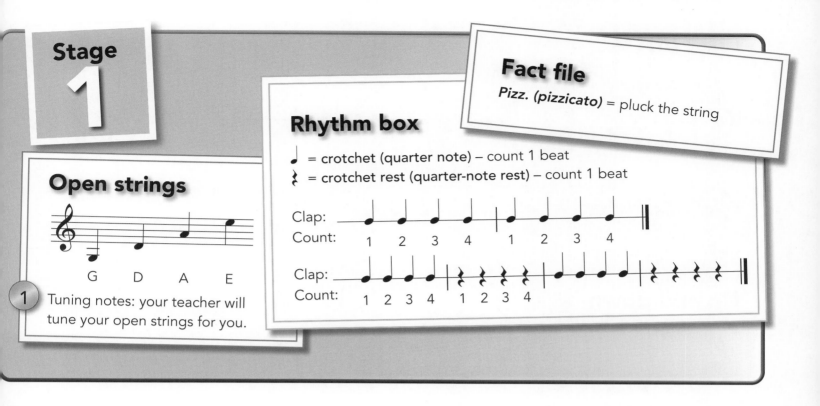

G D A E

① Tuning notes: your teacher will tune your open strings for you.

Rhythm box

♩ = crotchet (quarter note) – count 1 beat

𝄽 = crotchet rest (quarter-note rest) – count 1 beat

Clap:

Count: 1 2 3 4 1 2 3 4

Clap:

Count: 1 2 3 4 1 2 3 4

Fact file

Pizz. (pizzicato) = pluck the string

Warm-ups

Before you play

Head, shoulders, knees and toes
With your fingertips, tap your head, shoulders, knees then toes four times each. Repeat, tapping each three times, then two and finally once each.

Polishing the neck
In rest position, slide your left hand up and down the neck of the violin.

Getting ready to play

Put your violin up ready to play, with your left hand on the front right shoulder of the violin. You won't need your bow yet. Pluck (pizz.) all the pieces in this stage. Your right thumb should be tucked under the corner of the fingerboard.

Going up!

pizz.

Going down!

pizz.

Blast off!

Explosively!

Count each rest out loud

1 2 3 4

Up and down

Energetically

Superhero challenge

Go from rest position to playing position three times, silently.

(2) ## There's a hole-in my viol-in

Confidently

Top tip

Stand tall with your feet slightly apart and arms relaxed.

(3) ## I've run out of rosin

Sadly

4 March of the open strings 🎹

March-like

5 Secret agent on a mission 🎹

Secretly

Top tip

Repeat all these pieces plucking with the left-hand little finger at the high dot level on each string.

Activity box

☐ **Floating violin** Hold your violin above your head with your left-hand fingers around the high dot. Slide the tail button past your nose and down onto your collarbone, ending up in playing position. Repeat a few times.

☐ Name the strings and write them on the stave.

☐ **Make up your own piece** using G, D, A and E; it can be any length you like. You can either memorise it or write the notes down on the stave below. Remember to give it title.

_____ by _____

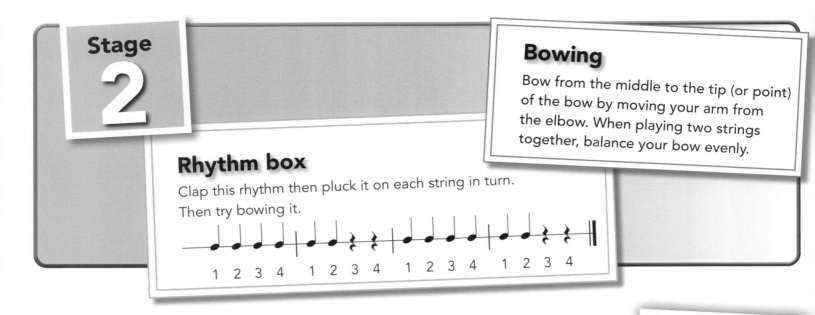

Rhythm box

Clap this rhythm then pluck it on each string in turn.
Then try bowing it.

1 2 3 4   1 2 3 4   1 2 3 4   1 2 3 4

Bowing

Bow from the middle to the tip (or point) of the bow by moving your arm from the elbow. When playing two strings together, balance your bow evenly.

Warm-ups

Before you play

Windscreen wipers
Holding your bow at the heel with your right hand, place the left hand lightly around the right wrist. Wave the tip of the bow in an arc, like a windscreen wiper. How many wipes can you do in a row, keeping a good bow hold? Keep a record.

Bouncing fingers
In playing position, with your fingers near the high dot, bounce all four fingers up and down on each string. Notice how your left arm rotates but your violin stays still.

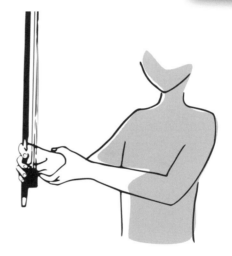

Top tip

Move your bow to the next string in the rests.

Warm-up

Not too fast

5

Scary...

Slowly

Johann Sebastian Bach comes to tea

With biscuits

Two by two

Slowly

Top tip

March your feet in the rests.

Marching energetically to your violin lesson

Marching energetically

Follow my lead

Lively

5

Hoe down

With lots of energy

5

Top tip

At the end of this piece lift your bow off the string dramatically!

Activity box

- ♩ is called a _____ and is worth _____ beat.

- 𝄽 is called a _____ and is worth _____ beat.

- **Without your violin or bow**   Bend your knees and gently 'bounce' up and down. Then, with feet shoulder-width apart, sway gently from side to side.

- **Stir the witches' cauldron**   Hold the bow with your best bow hold, with the tip pointing up. Draw circles with the heel, as if stirring a pot, changing direction every now and then. Name some horrible things to put in it!

- **Make up your own piece**   You can either memorise it or write down on the stave. If you need help ask your teacher. Remember to give your piece a title.

_____ by _____

Stage 3

Fact file

- п = **down-bow,** move your arm away from the violin
- ∨ = **up-bow,** move your arm towards the violin
- **Arco** = played with the bow
- *mf* = *mezzo forte* = quite loud
- *f* = *forte* = loud

Rhythm box

- ♩ = minim (half note) – count 2 beats
- ▬ = minim rest (half-note rest) – count 2 beats

Clap, pluck then bow these rhythms, each on a different string.

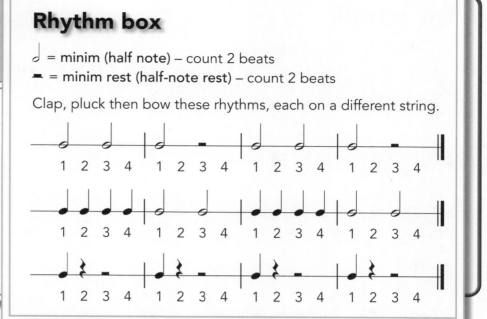

Before you play

- Lift your shoulders up towards your ears and then drop them down slowly.
- Hold straight arms out to the side and draw big circles in the air in both directions.
- Go from rest position to playing position three times silently.

Top tip

Move the bow more slowly for ♩

8 **Procession of the violin teachers**

Respectfully

A pizz of cake

Scrumptiously

15

9 Lift off!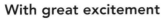

Top tip
Start each note at the point with a straight arm.

With great excitement

10 Keeping cool

Velvety

Blue circles in the air

Quite quickly

At the end of bars 2 and 4 draw a circle in the air
with your bow hand, ready to begin the next note.

11 The tortoise and the hare

Like a tortoise

Like a hare

Tortoise again

Hare again

12 At the palace

Regally

Have a rest

Calmly

L.H. pizz.

arco

mf

5 L.H. pizz.

arco

Top tip
Keep your left hand near the high dot to play these notes left-hand pizz.

Activity box

WORD SEARCH

Find the following words in this word search:

BOW
BRIDGE
CELLO
DOUBLE BASS
GUITAR
HAIR
HARP
PEGS
PIZZICATO
STICK
STRINGS
TIP
TUNER
VIOLA
VIOLIN

R	Y	F	P	H	F	W	J	V	O
B	B	R	I	D	G	E	I	I	Q
O	S	U	Z	T	I	C	P	O	T
W	T	X	Z	I	G	E	E	L	T
S	R	V	I	P	U	L	G	I	U
T	I	I	C	M	I	L	S	N	N
I	N	O	A	X	T	O	T	G	E
C	G	L	T	Q	A	H	A	I	R
K	S	A	O	Y	R	H	A	R	P
D	O	U	B	L	E	B	A	S	S

☐ 𝅗𝅥 is called a _____ and is worth _____ beats.

  𝄼 is called a _____ and is worth _____ beats.

☐ Choose your favourite string and bow it as many times as you can with your best tone quality and best bow hold.
Personal best: write down the number of repetitions with a good bow hold _____

☐ **Make up your own piece using** ♩ and 𝅗𝅥. Make it a cheerful piece and remember to give it a title.

_____ by _____

17

Stage 4

Rhythm box

Clap and pluck this rhythm, then bow it on each string in turn.

Fact file

- *Moderato* = play at a moderate speed
- *Andante* = play at a walking pace
- A **time signature** is the two numbers at the beginning of a piece. The top number tells you how many beats there are in a bar. $\frac{4}{4}$ has four ♩ beats in a bar

Warm-ups

Before you play

Circles: without your violin and bow, stretch your arms out in front of you and gently rotate your wrists in both directions eight times.

Goose neck: with your violin in playing position, lift your head slightly away from the chinrest and move it from side to side. Lightly move back into playing position. Is your neck relaxed?

Spiders: make a bow hold and point the tip of the bow to the ceiling. Wriggle your fingers and thumb to climb up the bow like a spider. Try coming back down again if you can. Be careful not to touch the hair!

Warm-up 1

Use short bows on the ♩ and long bows on the ♩

Warm-up 2

Bow from the middle to the tip, opening and closing the elbow.

18

13 Push and pull 🎹

Andante

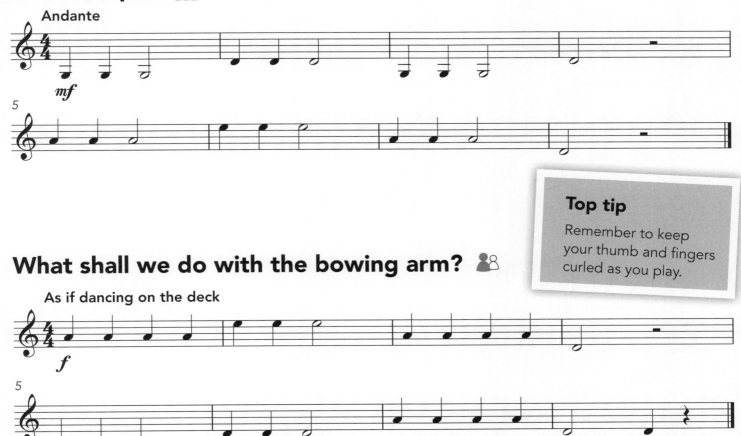

What shall we do with the bowing arm? 👥

As if dancing on the deck

> **Top tip**
>
> Remember to keep your thumb and fingers curled as you play.

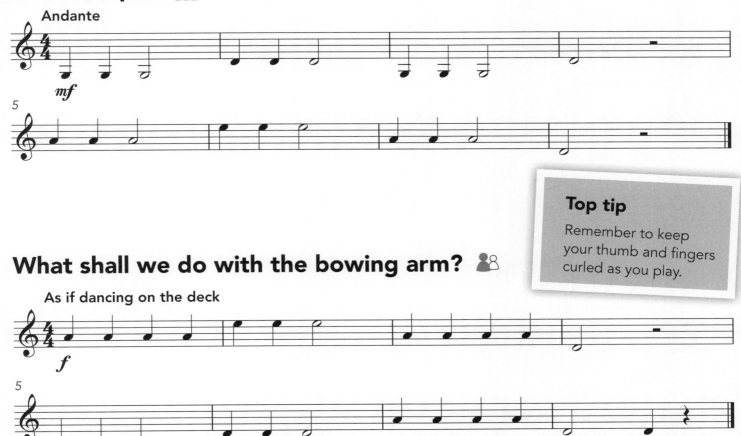

14 A calm picnic under the chestnut tree 🎹

Snoozingly

221B Rodeo Drive 👥

With a swing

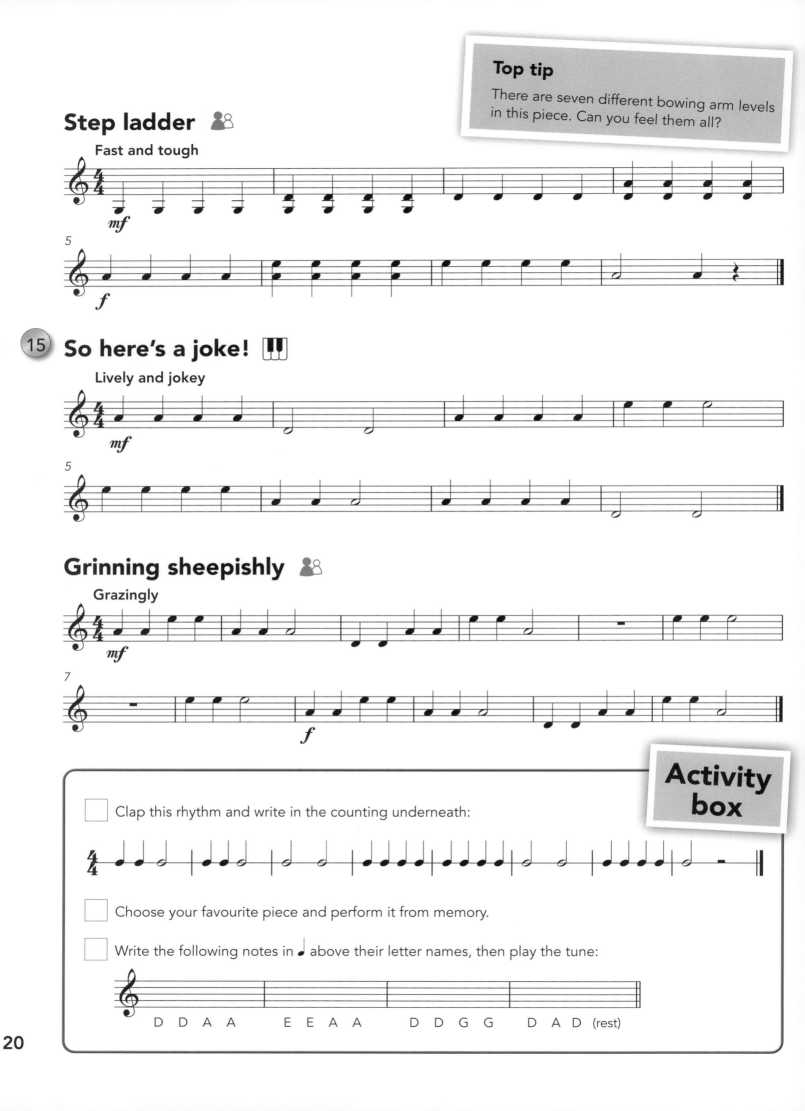

Step ladder

Fast and tough

Top tip
There are seven different bowing arm levels in this piece. Can you feel them all?

15 So here's a joke!

Lively and jokey

Grinning sheepishly

Grazingly

Activity box

☐ Clap this rhythm and write in the counting underneath:

☐ Choose your favourite piece and perform it from memory.

☐ Write the following notes in ♩ above their letter names, then play the tune:

D D A A   E E A A   D D G G   D A D (rest)

20

Stage 5

New notes

4 4

D A

Rhythm box

o = semibreve (whole note) – count 4 beats

Clap these rhythms, then pluck and bow them on the D and A strings.

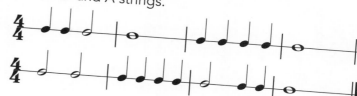

Fact file

o = **harmonic** = touch the string very lightly with the left little finger on the high dot to play these harmonics.

p = *piano* = quiet

Before you play

Holding the violin with your best posture, place your fourth finger lightly on the high dot on the D string and then A string to play these new notes. Keep your hand here in all the pieces in this stage.

Warm-ups

Top tip

The bow will need to move quite quickly for the harmonics.

16 **Chinese green tea**

Without milk

p

Top tip 1

Think about breathing gently in this piece. Keep your body relaxed.

17 ## A breath of fresh air

Slowly

mf

Frère Jacques 👥

After Gustav Mahler

Sadly

p

Haunted house 👥

Scarily

p

Top tip 2

Put some rosin on the bow and hold the bow lightly when playing harmonics.

Activity box

☐ 𝅝 is called a _____ and is worth _____ beats.

☐ Make up your own piece you could play at Christmas. Remember to give it a title.

_____ by _____

Stage 6

Fact file

- 𝄐 **pause** = hold the note for longer than its written value
- 𝄿 *tremolando* = a 'trembling effect', moving the bow very fast at the point

First finger E and B

E   B

Warm-ups

Before you play

Mousehole: in playing position, place your left thumb opposite the first finger. Can you make a tunnel of your hand under the fingerboard?

Finger tapper: this gets your left-hand fingers in the correct position – you won't need your bow. On the A string, hold down your first, second, third and fourth fingers – your teacher will show you where. Then tap your **first finger** up and down eight times. Repeat on the D string.

Singing practice: try singing to match your fingers to the tuning. Your teacher will sing A and B, then you have a go.

```
G  D  Ⓐ  E
      Ⓑ
      C♯
      Ⓓ
      Ⓔ
```

Stepping up

Stepping carefully

(18) ## Ghoulish goulash

Deliciously devilish

trem.

23

Top tip 1

Sing the pieces in this stage before playing them. Try to match your tuning to your singing.

19 ## Chicken, sweet and sour 🎹

Moderately, with lots of spice

20 ## Dreaming of summer 🎹

Hazily

21 ## The witch's curse 🎹

Spookily

Top tip 2

Gently slide up in bars 2 and 6, coming back down in bar 4. Check that your left thumb stays relaxed.

Busy teacher! 👥

Confidently

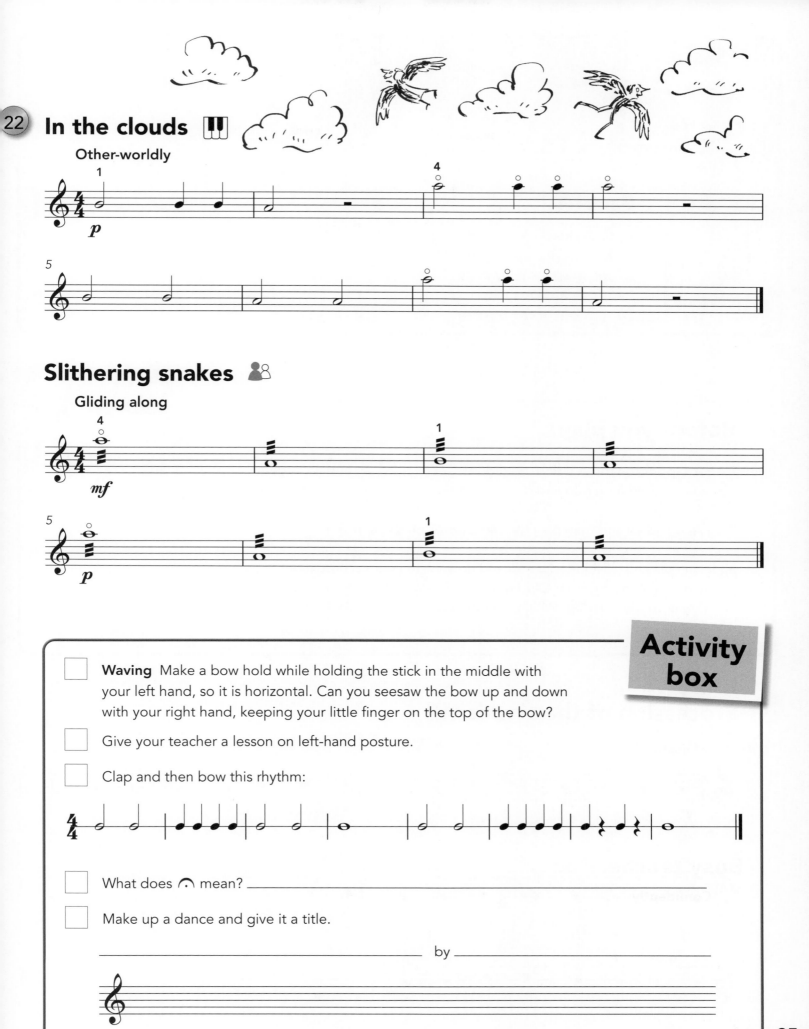

22 ## In the clouds 🎹

Other-worldly

Slithering snakes 👥

Gliding along

☐ **Waving** Make a bow hold while holding the stick in the middle with your left hand, so it is horizontal. Can you seesaw the bow up and down with your right hand, keeping your little finger on the top of the bow?

☐ Give your teacher a lesson on left-hand posture.

☐ Clap and then bow this rhythm:

☐ What does 𝑛 mean? _____

☐ Make up a dance and give it a title.

_____ by _____

25

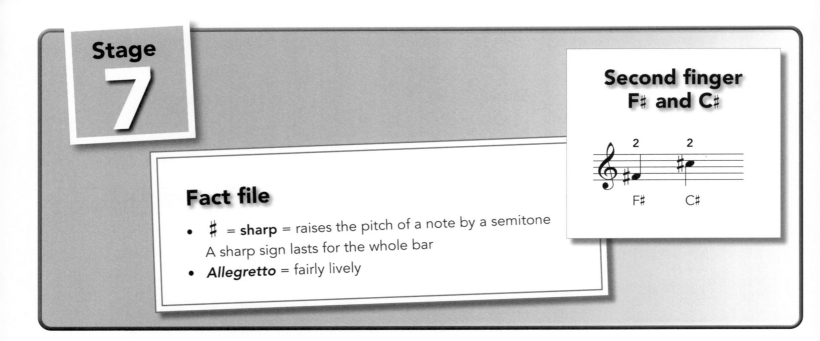

Stage 7

Second finger F♯ and C♯

Fact file

- ♯ = **sharp** = raises the pitch of a note by a semitone
  A sharp sign lasts for the whole bar
- *Allegretto* = fairly lively

Before you play

Finger tapper: on the A string, hold down your 1ˢᵗ, 2ⁿᵈ, 3ʳᵈ and 4ᵗʰ fingers. Tap your second finger up and down eight times. Repeat on the D string.

Sing A, B and C♯ and then play the same notes on the A string.

Slides: in playing position, slide up and down with your second finger lightly on the A string, from C♯ to the high dot position and back again. Then try it on the D string. Which note do you start on, and which note is the harmonic?

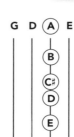

23. Procession of the scrolls

24 ## Dance in a trance 🎹

25 ## Mango tango 🎹

Top tip
Memorise this piece then perform it without the music.

26 ## Sally's sheep go astraying 🎹

North Cornish traditional

Top tip
Try singing this before you play it.

27 Merrily we roll out of bed

Traditional

Exceedingly merrily

Soda bread

Irish traditional

Reel-y fast

Activity box

☐ Fill in the missing word: a sharp (♯) _____ a note by a semitone.

☐ **Snakes!** Slide your second finger up and down the A string, then add the bow to make a slithering sound. Repeat with other fingers on other strings.

☐ Make up a piece using all the notes you have learnt so far. Try to include some dynamics (loud or quiet markings). Write it down then play it.

_____ by _____

28

Fact file

- *Allegro* = lively
- *mp* = *mezzo piano* = quite quiet

G   D

Warm-ups

Sing D, E, F♯, G and then play this exercise. Listen to the tuning of each note, and match your third finger to the open string.

1.

Now sing A, B, C♯, D and then play this exercise on the A string, listening to the tuning again.

2.

Double trouble

Can you spot the connection between the two lines?

28 ## Fast food rag

Top tip

Lift your bow back to the heel in the rests.

29

Top tip

Can you play this whole piece with softly curved right fingers and thumb?

29 ## The bells

French traditional

Moderato and ringing

30 ## Sword dance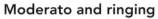

Thoinot Arbeau

Moderato and rather carefully!

A BAD piece

Why is this a bad piece?

Badly

31 ## The sun shines hot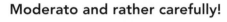

Estonian traditional

Allegretto with sunscreen (factor 30)

32 Old MacDonald had a farm 🎹

Traditional

Allegro

mf   *f*

mf   *f*

mf

f

Top tip
Can you perform this piece from memory?

Activity box

☐ What can you find out about a (musical) rag?

☐ Can you name some other string instruments? _____

☐ Clap, and then bow this rhythm:

☐ **Squeezy!** Squeeze your whole body very tightly – even your face! Then relax like jelly.

☐ Make up a piece using all the notes on the D and A strings.

_____ by _____

Stage 9

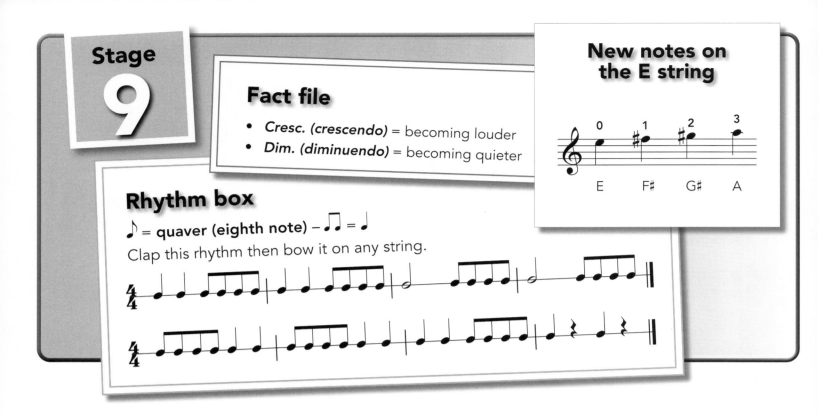

Fact file

- *Cresc. (crescendo)* = becoming louder
- *Dim. (diminuendo)* = becoming quieter

New notes on the E string

E   F#   G#   A

Rhythm box

♪ = **quaver (eighth note)** – ♫ = ♩

Clap this rhythm then bow it on any string.

Warm-ups

Play this with long bows and concentrate on keeping your bowing arm relaxed. How many seconds can you play each note for? Keep a note of your personal best.

1.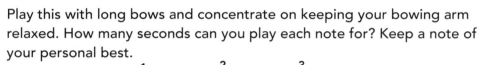

Personal best

Date	Seconds

Use less bow for the quavers (eighth notes):

2.

The quavers in bars 1 and 3 will be in the top half of the bow. Where will they be in bars 2 and 4?

3.

Listen to your sound on the long notes: check there are no wobbles.

4.

Apple pie and ice cream

Yummily

Apple pie and custard

Deliciously

Jolly holly

Exceedingly festive

33

Jingle bells

Dashing festively through the snow

James Pierpont

Top tip

This piece is best played all on the A string, so try using 4th finger for E.

33

34 Pony ride on a warm spring day 🎹

Allegretto

p

mf   *dim.*

35 The old musical box 🎹

Tunefully

mf

p   *cresc.*

p   *cresc.*

mf

Activity box

☐ **Relaxation technique** This is an excellent exercise to do before a performance. Breathe in through your nose while counting to four, then out through your mouth while counting to six. As you repeat this, notice how it helps to relax your body and improve concentration.

☐ Clap, then bow this rhythm:

☐ Choose a piece from the book and invent your own title for it. Then play it in the mood to fit your title. Perform it and ask your audience to guess your title.

Stage 10

New notes on the G string

G   A   B   C   D

Scale of G major

Fact file

- *Lento* = quite slow
- **Key signature** = the sharps or flats at the beginning of a piece tell you what key the piece is in. G major has a key signature of one sharp. A scale is made up of the notes of the key. Scales are fun!

Warm-ups

Start with your bow at the point on the E string and lift the bow in the air as soon as you've played the short E. Land on the G and relax. Think about how your arm moves.

1.

This exercise helps get your arms in the right position for playing on the G string.

2.

This exercise contains a new G string harmonic. Aim to keep your left elbow at the same angle through the piece.

3.

Top tip

You will need to swing both elbows into position in the rest.

Start this warm-up in the middle of the bow. Play it quite fast and work out how the dynamic changes affect the amount of bow you use.

4.
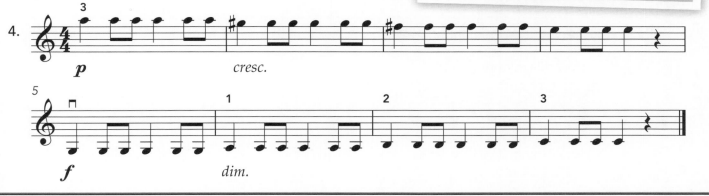

Top tip 1

The next pieces are all in G major.
Remember that the Fs are F sharps.

Top tip 2

Swing both arms in the rests
to prepare the next string.

Top tip 3

Fourth fingers help to avoid string
crossings if used instead of open strings.

Key time

36 Good King Wenceslas

Traditional

Violin boogie

37 Floating in the wind

36

Steam train

Chugging along

PRACTICE MAP

Here's a 'Practice Map' for your first practice of *Steam train*. Think about different ways you can mix and match the ingredients, then have fun practising them! Try making up your own Practice Map for other pieces.

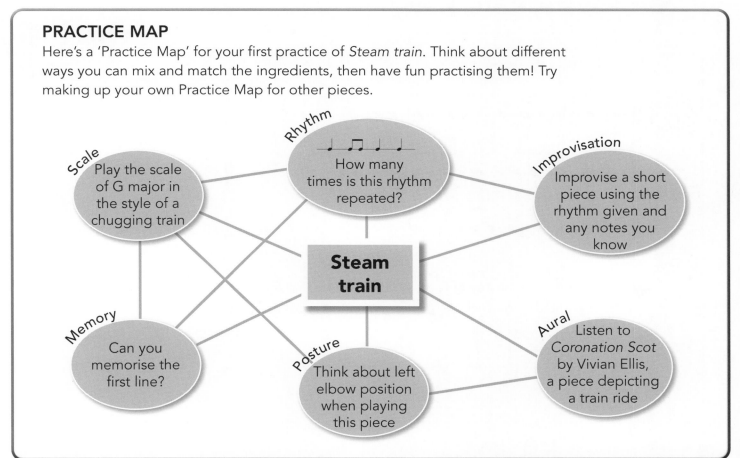

Scale
Play the scale of G major in the style of a chugging train

Rhythm
How many times is this rhythm repeated?

Improvisation
Improvise a short piece using the rhythm given and any notes you know

Steam train

Memory
Can you memorise the first line?

Posture
Think about left elbow position when playing this piece

Aural
Listen to *Coronation Scot* by Vivian Ellis, a piece depicting a train ride

Weightlifting

Heavily (don't drop the weights)

(39) The road to Humpybong

With spirit

Australian traditional

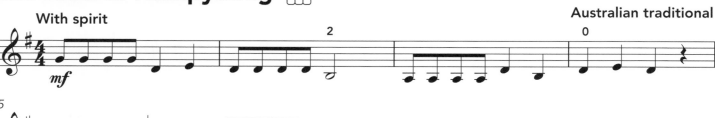

Activity box

☐ Clap then bow these rhythms:

☐ Make up a piece in the key of G major using all the fingers on the G and D strings. Include ♫♫ and this rhythm: ♩ 𝄾 ♩

_____ by _____

Stage

11

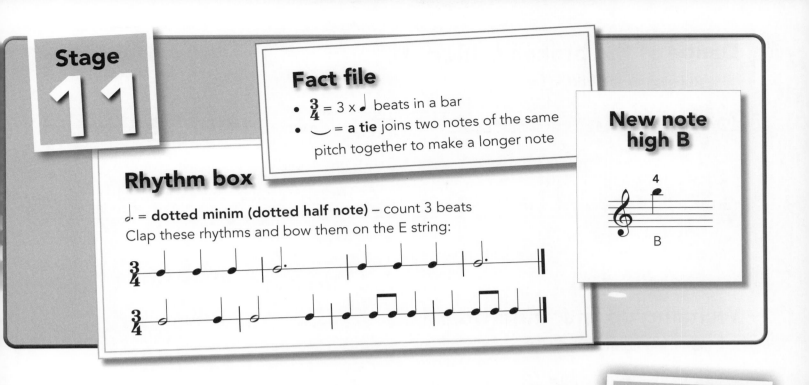

Fact file

- $\frac{3}{4}$ = 3 x ♩ beats in a bar
- ⌣ = **a tie** joins two notes of the same pitch together to make a longer note

New note high B

4

B

Rhythm box

♩. = **dotted minim (dotted half note)** – count 3 beats
Clap these rhythms and bow them on the E string:

Warm-ups

Try this in the usual way, holding down the 1ˢᵗ, 2ⁿᵈ and 3ʳᵈ fingers and tapping with your fourth.

1.

Swing your left elbow when changing strings so that the fourth finger is comfortable.

2.

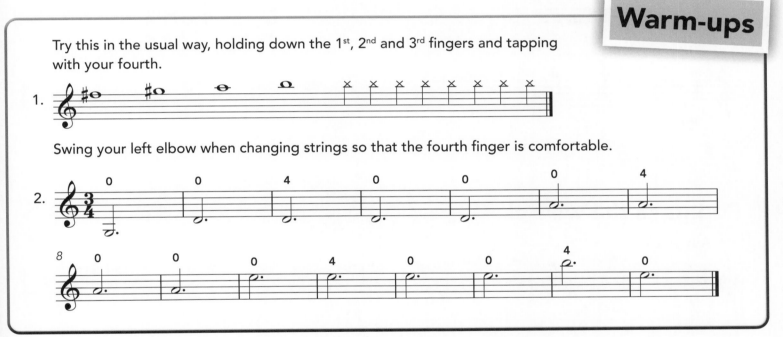

Play it again, Sam! 👥

Repetitively

A repeat mark = play again

mf

Top tip

Lift the up-bows right off the string!

(40) **Hicc-up** 🎹

Annoyingly

f

39

41 Dance of the broken bridge

Running to the bridge shop

Waltzing up the fingerboard

Dancing lightly

> **Top tip 1**
> Keep your left wrist relaxed and fingers curled.

42 Pop goes the weasel

Allegretto

Traditional

> **Top tip 2**
> Can you perform this from memory?

Pop!

> How many ties can you spot in this piece?

43 Daisy, Daisy

Harry Dacre

Moderato

CROSSWORD

Across

2. Playing the violin is lots of _____
5. Do it again.
7. Enjoyable patterns that go up and down.
11. Indicates you play more than one note in a bow.
12. Virtuosic Italian violinist with curly hair, born in 1782.
14. Play with the bow.
15. Becoming louder.
16. A shivering sound at the point of the bow.

Down

1. Hold this note longer (usually at the end of a piece).
3. Strings and washing are held by these.
4. Playing short notes on the string.
6. Using your fingers rather than your bow.
8. What you carry your violin in.
9. This raises a note by a semitone.
10. Play with a bouncing bow.
13. Fast and lively.

☐ **Violin gym** Stretch your fingers straight out for three seconds and then relax for three seconds. Repeat three times.

☐ **Tremolando** Play a scale of G major, holding every note for three beats, with a *tremolando* on every note. What effect does the *tremolando* have on the sound?

☐ Clap then bow this rhythm:

☐ Make up a tune using this rhythm and give it a title connected with 'three' (such as triangle, tripod or perhaps your three favourite ice cream flavours!).

_____ by _____

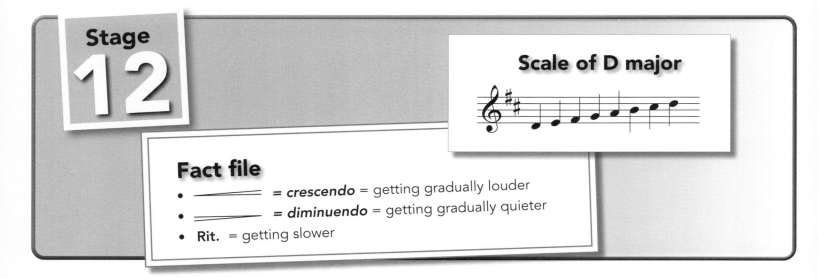

Stage 12

Scale of D major

Fact file

- ——— = *crescendo* = getting gradually louder
- ——— = *diminuendo* = getting gradually quieter
- **Rit.** = getting slower

Warm-ups

Before you play

Finger tapper: put all four fingers on the D string, then lift the fourth finger up and down eight times.

Bouncing: put all four fingers down together on the E string near the high dot and bounce them up and down eight times. Repeat on the A, D and G strings, noticing how the left elbow moves.

Top tip

Keep your fourth finger curled when you use it.

(44) ## Song of the happy frog

Happily

Japanese traditional

(45) ## Song of the Tanuki

Boisterously

Japanese traditional

49 Twinkle twinkle little app

Allegretto

mf

5

4   4

9

Twinkle twinkle little app
How I wonder where to tap!
Now it's crashed – that's quite a trick:
So it's just a plastic brick.
Twinkle twinkle little app,
Can you hear my patience snap?

Words by Sam Edenborough

50 When the saints go marching in

Moderato   American traditional

V   4

f

6

12

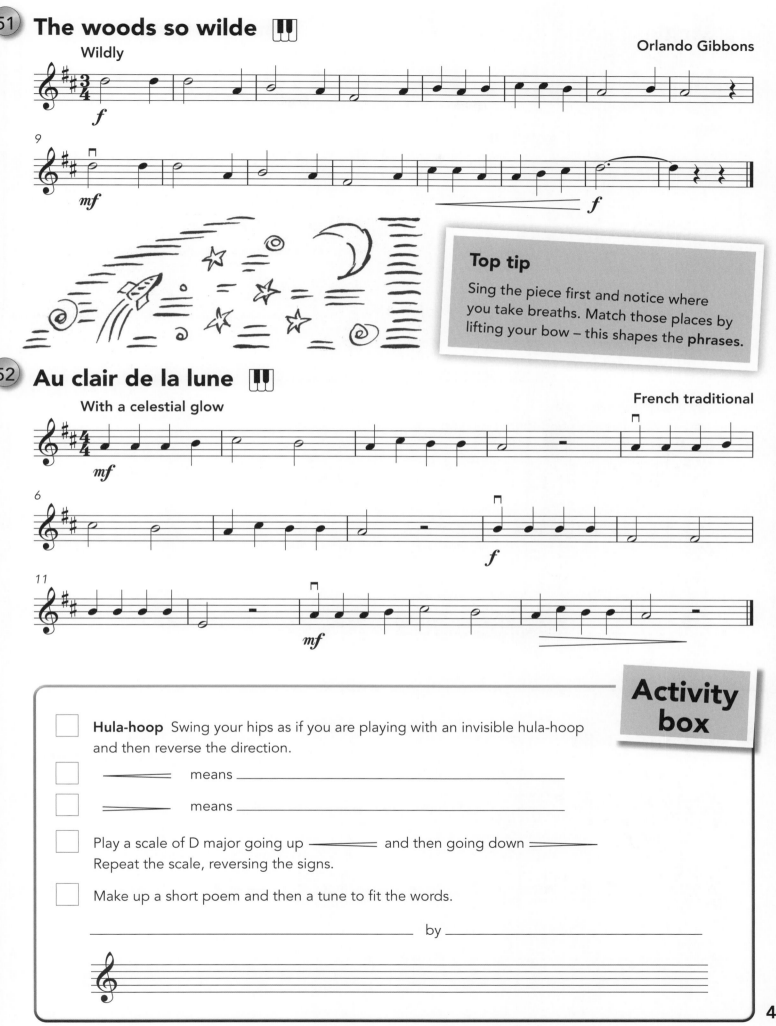

51 The woods so wilde

Wildly

Orlando Gibbons

Top tip

Sing the piece first and notice where you take breaths. Match those places by lifting your bow – this shapes the **phrases.**

52 Au clair de la lune

With a celestial glow

French traditional

Activity box

☐ **Hula-hoop** Swing your hips as if you are playing with an invisible hula-hoop and then reverse the direction.

☐ ⎯⎯ means _____

☐ ⎯⎯ means _____

☐ Play a scale of D major going up ⎯⎯ and then going down ⎯⎯ Repeat the scale, reversing the signs.

☐ Make up a short poem and then a tune to fit the words.

_____ by _____

Stage 13

Fact file

$\frac{2}{4}$ = 2 x ♩ beats in a bar

Scale and arpeggio of A major

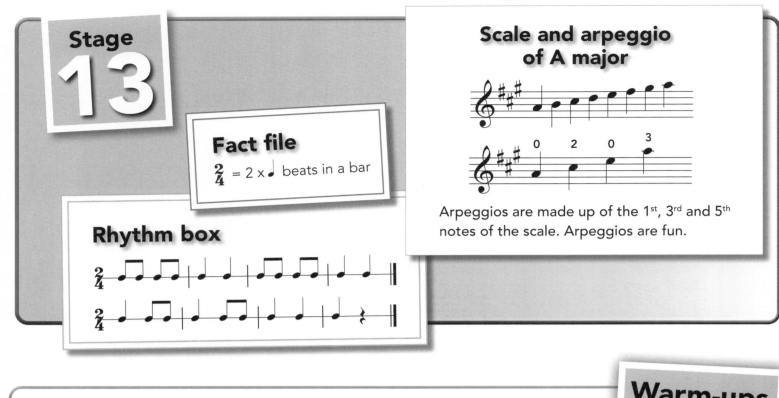

Arpeggios are made up of the 1st, 3rd and 5th notes of the scale. Arpeggios are fun.

Rhythm box

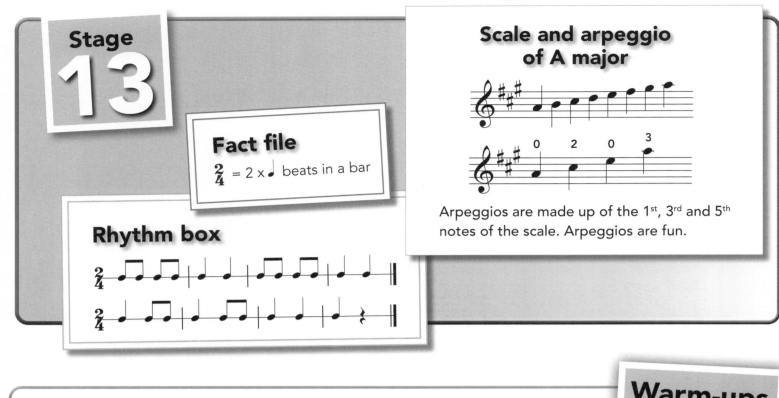

Warm-ups

Play this quite slowly, using the middle to the point of the bow and keeping your left wrist and thumb relaxed.

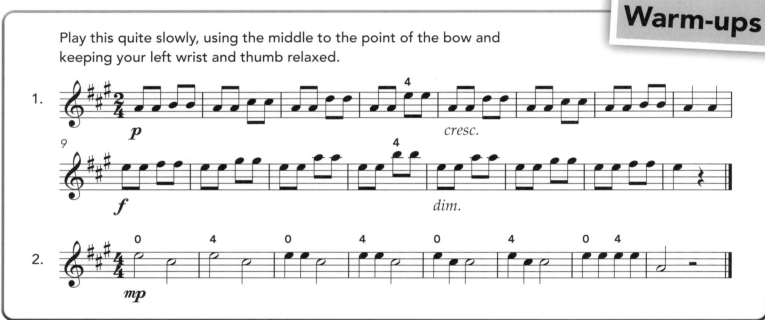

53 Ode to joy

Ludwig van Beethoven

Lightly bow

Sprightly and politely

German traditional

Song of the wind

German traditional

Slowly and blowly

Morning has broken (but not my violin)

Scottish traditional

With that waking up feeling

Waltzing to school

Swayingly

mf

56 Cuckoo

German traditional

Twitteringly

f

Activity box

☐ **See-saw** With your left hand near the high dot and your arm under the violin, swing your left elbow as far as possible to the left and then to the right. Gently repeat.

☐ **Breathing bow** Take a deep breath in then play a long down-bow, breathing out at the same time. Now try an up-bow, breathing in. Now repeat the down-bow. Make this a **Personal best** game. Can you make the bow and breath lengths longer each time? Keep a log of your progress and record the length in seconds.

☐ Make up a short tune and include an arpeggio of A major:

Personal best	
Date	Seconds

_____ by _____

48

Fact file

- **Slurs** ⌣ = a curved line joining notes of different pitches; play these notes in one bow
- *Espressivo* = expressively
- *Pesante* = heavily
- 𝄵 = **common time** = another way of writing a $\frac{4}{4}$ time signature
- *Poco rit.* = getting a little slower

Warm-ups

To slur these notes, put a sticker in the middle of your bow stick and change finger when you pass it. In the rests, stop the bow and prepare the next note.

Top tip 1

Change the finger gently under one bow, keeping an even tone quality.

This is called **legato** playing.

Top tip 2

Play this piece with separate bows first and then add the slurs.

Rhino

Andante pesante

Up the Nile

Egyptoso

57

Judge's dance

Swedish traditional

Allegretto

58

Violin concerto

Moderato espressivo

59

Aura Lee

American traditional

Andante espressivo

A Highland tale

With haggis and kilts

Top tip

Play this from the middle to the tip of the bow. How much quicker do you need to make the down-bows?

Waltz of the loose bow hairs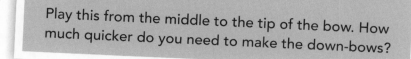

Allegretto

Activity box

☐ What is the difference between a slur and a tie? _____

_____

☐ Choose a favourite piece from earlier on in the book and perform it from memory.

☐ **Air playing** Play a piece with an imaginary violin and bow and very loose arms. Try to keep that feeling when you're holding your real violin and bow.

☐ Make up a piece in G major using just the G and D strings and include some slurs.

_____ by _____

☐ Next play it a string higher – on D and A. What key is it in now? _____

Stage 15

Second octave scale and arpeggio of G major

New notes C on the A string and G on the E string are both played with a **low** (or close) **second finger**. This ⌐—⌐ means that the notes (and fingers) are close. The distance between them is called a **semitone**.

Fact file

- **>** = accent = play notes with extra weight
- *Giocoso* = happily or joyfully
- *Maestoso* = majestically
- **Up-beat** = a shortened introductory bar
- ♮ = **natural** = cancels a sharp or flat

Warm-ups

Before you play

This is a silent warm-up. With a relaxed left wrist, put the third finger on the D on the A string. Then put the second finger on C♯ and slide it backwards and forwards four times. With your third finger still in place, try moving the first finger in the same way.

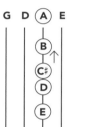

Top tip

Check the weight of the violin is balanced between the chin rest and shoulder – not just your left hand.

Up and down

Allegretto

Up high 👥

Andante espressivo

Tiger tango

Giocoso

f

Square dance round

With lots of shapes

mf

f

A round is a piece in which each player has the same melody but begins at a different time.

* Second player begins when first player reaches here.

62 Old bush song

Australian traditional

Moderato

f

4

mf

f

63 O come, all ye faithful

Traditional

Maestoso

mf

4

mp

4

p

poco rit.

mf

f

Top tip

Hold the bow lightly to give the bird-like character.

(64) The bird catcher's song

Allegro moderato

Wolfgang Amadeus Mozart

Rock solid

Steady rock tempo

Activity box

☐ **Stand tall** Imagine someone is gently pulling one of your hairs from the top of your head towards the ceiling. Can you feel yourself getting taller? Now drop your shoulders but keep your neck and back very relaxed.

☐ **Magic** Holding your bow with a good bow hold, use the point to perform spells like a wizard. Don't hit anything! What might these spells do: 'slurissimo pegitis', 'skickellius tremioso' and 'frogata dottilium'?

☐ Make up a piece in G major (using both octaves) starting on an upbeat.

_____ by _____

Scale and arpeggio of E natural minor

E minor has the same key signature as G major.

Fact file

- *ff* = *fortissimo* = very loud
- ꞌ = *staccato* = play the note short and crisply
- *Vivace* = lively

Top tip

Short notes can be played two ways:
Staccato: play in the upper half of the bow, on the string, stopping and starting the bow.
Spiccato: play in the lower half of the bow, finding the balance point where the bow bounces naturally.

Warm-ups

'Appy arpeggios

Dinosaur park

Lento monsterioso

Top tip 1
Play this piece staccato first, then spiccato.

Top tip 2
2 = 2 bars' rest

65 Things that go bump in the night

Creepily

66 Mountain stream

Henry Lazarus

Flowing

cresc.

poco rit.

56

67 **Sonata in E minor** 🎹

Top tip
Listen to the echoes in the piano part in the rests.

Allegro moderato

68 **Pepperoni plus** 🎹

Fast and spicy

Activity box

☐ **Waving** With an excellent bowhold and the left hand supporting the stick in the middle, seesaw the bow up and down with your right hand.

☐ **Pain in the neck!** Without your violin, slowly look to the right and then the left. Keep your body still and your neck relaxed. Repeat a few times.

☐ Make up a piece in E minor, including some staccato notes.

_____ by _____

Stage 17

Rhythm box

♩. = dotted crotchet (dotted quarter note)

♩. = ♪ + ♪ + ♪ or ♩ + ♪

Clap then bow these rhythms on the A string:

Warm-ups

Square dance 👥

Round dance

Allegretto

mf

Top tip
Lift the up-bows lightly and quickly.

Roundabout

Without falling off

mf

* Play as a round with second player starting when the first player reaches here.

69 Deck the halls

Welsh traditional

Allegretto

f

mf

poco rit.

f

59

Stage 18

Fact file

Andantino = slightly faster than andante

Warm-ups

Keep your first finger on the string while your second finger slides.

1.

2.

3.

4.

Top tip

Play the first note, then sing the tune before you play the piece.

71 **Happy birthday**

With a very big slice of cake

Patty and Mildred Hill

72 **Homage to JSB**

Allegro moderato

Top tip

Play in the top half of the bow to give a stylish effect.

73 **Greensleeves**

Andante

English traditional

74 **Hornpipe**

Nautically

Humming song

Robert Schumann

Andantino

Extra large brown jug

J.E. Winner

75

Allegro con spirito

☐ **Recital time** Choose three or four of your favourite pieces and give a recital to family and friends. Make a programme containing the titles of each piece and a few words about you. Wear your best concert clothes! Record your recital if you can – you'll enjoy listening to it in the future.

☐ For your final composition or improvisation why not make up a musical picture of your violin teacher.

Well done!

_____

has successfully completed
Violin Basics